Little Laureates

Merseyside

Edited by Angela Fairbrace

YoungWriters
First published in Great Britain in 2007 by:
Young Writers
Remus House
Coltsfoot Drive
Peterborough
PE2 9JX
Telephone: 01733 890066
Website: www.youngwriters.co.uk

SB ISBN 978-1 84431 097 5

Foreword

Young Writers was established in 1991 and has been passionately devoted to the promotion of reading and writing in children and young adults ever since. The quest continues today. Young Writers remains as committed to the nurturing of poetic and literary talent as ever.

This year's Young Writers competition has proven as vibrant and dynamic as ever and we are delighted to present a showcase of the best poetry from across the UK and in some cases overseas. Each poem has been selected from a wealth of *Little Laureates* entries before ultimately being published in this, our sixteenth primary school poetry series.

Once again, we have been supremely impressed by the overall quality of the entries we have received. The imagination, energy and creativity which has gone into each young writer's entry made choosing the poems a challenging and often difficult but ultimately hugely rewarding task - the general high standard of the work submitted ensured this opportunity to bring their poetry to a larger appreciative audience.

We sincerely hope you are pleased with this final collection and that you will enjoy *Little Laureates Merseyside* for many years to come.

Contents

The Poems

The Magic Box

(Based on 'Magic Box' by Kit Wright)

I have a magic box . . .
It will double anything like socks
Or sometimes it will give me something new
Like my dear old aunty Soo
A picture of my mum and dad
A memory of being bad.

A memory of a baby calf
While I'm wearing a lilac scarf
The sound of a unicorn cantering around
As a fairy flutters to the ground.

My box is gold and red
And it sits beside my bed
And now my poem comes to an end
But if you ever need a friend
I'll be just around the bend.

Kirsty Rimmer (9)

Silence Is . . .

Sounds like nothing
Feels like a hard floor
Tastes of cold air blowing around everywhere
It smells like mist
It looks like empty sky and grass
it is green, white and blue
It reminds me of an empty field
Silence is everywhere.

Tia Birks (7)
Arrowe Hill Primary School

Sadness Is . . .

Sadness sounds like a gunshot ringing in an alleyway.
Sadness feels like eyedrops running down your cheeks.
Sadness tastes like salty water.
Sadness smells like a rotten banana.
Sadness looks like clear water.
Sadness reminds me of my two brothers fighting outside of my house.
You don't want to be *sad*,
Do you?

Joe Atherton (8)
Arrowe Hill Primary School

Happiness

Happiness sounds like children at a party
Happiness feels like a fluffy cushion
Happiness tastes like sweets
Happiness smells like strawberries
Happiness looks like a bright flower
Happiness reminds me of my puppy dog in a picture frame
Happiness is as pink as a pig.

Jade Jones (8)
Arrowe Hill Primary School

Fun

Fun sounds like people laughing
Fun reminds me of my friends playing football
Fun is children playing in a bathtub
Fun feels like fur going through your hands.

Jamie Conway (7)
Arrowe Hill Primary School

Fun

Fun is the sound of screaming and children having fun
Fun feels like excitement running all around you
It tastes like party food going mad in your mouth
Fun smells like a tasty cooked barbecue waiting for you
Fun is children opening presents on Christmas Day
Fun reminds me of waking mums up on a Sunday morning
Fun is multicoloured.

Ellie Hill (8)
Arrowe Hill Primary School

Love

Love sounds like a bell ringing at a wedding
Love is a happy thing
Love reminds me of my nan getting married
Love is a good thing to share
Love is a gentle feeling
Love is beautiful.

Kyle Sutton (7)
Arrowe Hill Primary School

Darkness

The sound of a creaking window
It feels like smoky air
It tastes like liquorice
It smells like smoke coming from a fire
It looks like a big black cloud
It reminds me of a horror film.

Lee Jones (8)
Arrowe Hill Primary School

Love

L ove is when someone is gentle
O n Valentine's Day we give presents
V iciousness makes people scared
E veryone needs to feel love.

Chantelle Farrell (8)
Arrowe Hill Primary School

Love Is . . .

L ove is when you get married
O ther people can love each other
V ery old people have been loved a long time
E veryone needs love.

Paige Jones (7)
Arrowe Hill Primary School

Love

L is for lonely without you
O is on the way to your house
V is Valentine cards and gifts
E is enough to be with you.

Owen Liddicott (8)
Arrowe Hill Primary School

Fun

F un is when you laugh
U nder the tree while talking
N ear the treetops in the treehouse.

Dawn Parsons (8)
Arrowe Hill Primary School

Laughter

L aughing children in the distance
A lways playing and having fun
U nder and over the hills they go
G iggling and smiling all day long
H aving breaks to catch their breath
T alking and playing all the time
E ven when they go to sleep
R esting when they go to sleep.

Laura Jones (9)
Arrowe Hill Primary School

Sadness

S adness is when someone is nasty to another person
A nger is the sound of loud sadness
D arkness reminds me of the scary monster
N obody has fun when they are sad
E is the fifth letter in sadness
S adness is not what we feel in school
S adness is when you sometimes start to cry.

Rebecca Jones (7)
Arrowe Hill Primary School

Darkness Is . . .

D arkness is scary
A ll is quiet and time for bed
R aining and dark, I can't see
K eep warm, snuggle up
E nemies you see but they are not there
S ilence all
S ilence all.

Becky Penfold (7)
Arrowe Hill Primary School

Laughter

L aughing all day
A nd all night
U nder the quilt
G oing to be a naughty girl, I see
H aving chocolates
T hat's too sweet
E ating them up
R eady to go to sleep.

Lauran Jones (9)
Arrowe Hill Primary School

Anger

A is for arguing
N is for naughty
G is for going out of the house
E is for echoing shouts
R is for running away from home
You don't want to be where anger is!

Christian Rule (9)
Arrowe Hill Primary School

Love

L is for loving
O is for out on a date
V is for violin
E is for eating.

Matthew Robinson (8)
Arrowe Hill Primary School

Love

Love is the sound of happiness
Love feels like a warm heart inside you
Love smells like fresh air all around you
Love looks like a happy thing
Love reminds me of people buying me presents
The colour of love is red.

Olivia Wilkie (7)
Arrowe Hill Primary School

Hunger

H is for hungry
U is for upset tum
N is for nibbling
G is for grapes
E is for eating
R is for recipes.

Ryan Halligan (8)
Arrowe Hill Primary School

Love

L means loving someone
O is for opening a shop
V is for Valentine chocolates
E is for eating.

Lewis Wright (7)
Arrowe Hill Primary School

Feelings

Hate is black like pitch darkness
It smells like a fire's ash
It feels like molten lava
It looks like a swollen blue river
It tastes like the water from a pool of envy
It sounds like an eerie echo
It reminds me of a raging thunderstorm.

Sophie Appleton (10)
Bleak Hill Primary School

Feelings

Happiness is red like a flame sparkling
It feels like sleeping on a bed of marshmallows
It smells like hot chocolate with marshmallows on top
It sounds like birds whistling in the air
It tastes like cookies and milk
It looks like a herd of horses galloping free
It reminds me of the hot blazing sun.

Emily Ball (9)
Bleak Hill Primary School

Feelings

Anger is grey like a foggy morning
It feels like thick black oil
It sounds like crackling lightning and thunder
It smells like burning gases and ashes
It tastes like burning chillies
It reminds me of lava crashing through the earth.

Ryan Ashcroft (10)
Bleak Hill Primary School

Feelings

Love is red like sparkling jewels
It tastes like a ripe red cherry
It looks like a bright scarlet cloth
It sounds like water running down a stream
It smells like seven rosebuds
It feels like velvet rubbing on your skin
It reminds me of a bunch of roses.

Jack Bibby (10)
Bleak Hill Primary School

Feelings

Hate is as red as a burning fireplace
It looks like a rusty piece of metal
It smells like a sweaty envious monster
It feels like you're being bullied
It sounds like a drummer going out of control
It tastes like grotty eggs
Hate reminds me of the dazzling sun in the summer.

Alex Black (9)
Bleak Hill Primary School

Feelings

Hate is blue like the depths of the sea
It feels like a heart splitting in two
It looks like a bloody massacre
It smells like smoke rising from a fire
It tastes like a fire's ash
It sounds like lightning crackling
It reminds me of thunder booming.

Elizabeth Botcherby (10)
Bleak Hill Primary School

Feelings

Fear is white like horrid pain
It tastes like crushed mouldy aspirin
It looks like a painful storm
It sounds like pain shooting right through you
It feels like falling down a cliff
It smells like sour lemon juice
It reminds me of walking to the deputy head.

Louis Burdett (9)
Bleak Hill Primary School

Feelings

Anger is red as the beaming sun
It smells like burning oil
It sounds like a devil in your car
It looks like a boiling furnace in the dark
It feels like a bull in a bullring
It tastes like the hottest chilli
It reminds me of a wall of fire.

Adam Callan (9)
Bleak Hill Primary School

Feelings

Happiness is green like grass
Happiness looks like the light of a bright morning
Happiness feels like a settee of pillows
Happiness smells like roast chicken
Happiness sounds like a herd of horses neighing
Happiness tastes like fluffy marshmallows
Happiness reminds me of the shining sun.

Joshua Carr (10)
Bleak Hill Primary School

Feelings

Happiness is white like a sparkling moon
It smells like melted hot chocolate
It sounds like the swaying breeze in the air
It tastes like delicious candy sweets
It looks like a steaming hot sun
It feels like a plane blasting in the sky
Happiness reminds me of a shining moonlit night.

Tom Carr (9)
Bleak Hill Primary School

Feelings

Fear is white like cold icebergs
It feels like a jagged saw
It tastes like a frozen ice cream
It looks like a ghost in the dark of the night
It smells like a frozen snowy lake
It sounds like a crackling campfire
It reminds me of a cold snowy day.

Sam Cutayar (9)
Bleak Hill Primary School

Feelings

Love is red like a loving heart
It sounds like the sea's waves rushing to the dry sand
It tastes like chocolate shaped like a heart
It smells like rose petals growing on its lovely scented rose
It feels like running through luscious green grass
It looks like the sunset on a beach
It reminds me of the sun beaming on the sea.

Jessica Fenney (9)
Bleak Hill Primary School

Feelings

Sadness is black like a pirate's back
It looks like a sack of slack
It feels like your heart stopping
It smells like a party popper popping
It sounds like people lying
It tastes like neat vinegar
It reminds me of a baby crying.

Liam Jones (9)
Bleak Hill Primary School

Feelings

Sadness is blue like ice cubes falling
It feels like your tummy's crushing
It smells like friendship dying
It looks like a deep blue sea waving
It sounds like the clashing of loud lightning
It tastes like a dead piece of skin
It reminds me of an iceberg crashing.

Jessica Laughton (10)
Bleak Hill Primary School

Feelings

Love is pink like rosy-red cheeks
It looks like the sun setting across the sea
It sounds like a flute whistling its lovely tune
It tastes like a sugar cane, they make me jump with glee
It smells like lemon drizzle cake
It feels like the air weaving through my fingers
It reminds me of my first funfair ride.

Daniel Lea-Wilson (10)
Bleak Hill Primary School

Feelings

Sadness is grey like clouds floating
It smells like a pool of tears
It sounds like a heart breaking with a crack
It looks like a big broken heart
It tastes like a big bowl of evil
It feels like your heart breaking painfully
It reminds me of a lonely death.

Luke McLellan (10)
Bleak Hill Primary School

Feelings

Love is red like a rose
It tastes like nice sugary sweets
It smells like candles burning on a lovely night
It feels like rose petals floating down from the sky
It looks like big red hearts
It sounds like violins playing peacefully
It reminds me of romantic films on the TV.

Alex Naisbitt (10)
Bleak Hill Primary School

Feelings

Love is red like bright red roses
It sounds like a heart beating calmly
It feels like jumping into a pool of melted chocolate
It looks like a red heart gleaming in the light
It tastes like a bright rosy apple
It reminds me of glistening dark rubies.

Isabel Macbryde (10)
Bleak Hill Primary School

Feelings

Happiness is blue like the drifting sky
It tastes like chocolate melting in your mouth
It looks like the sun beaming in your eye
It feels like a bear cuddling you all night
It smells like roses falling all around you
It sounds like the wind drifting side to side
It reminds me of a holiday, peaceful and sunny.

Georgia Naylor (10)
Bleak Hill Primary School

Feelings

Fear is as white as a zombie's moaning face
It looks like a mouse being chased by a cat
It tastes like a fresh lemon being squeezed on your tongue
It feels like something inside you has exploded
It smells like rubbish being dumped at a landfill site
It sounds like a giant battle tank firing in war
It reminds me of a funeral and it will forever haunt me.

James O'Leary (10)
Bleak Hill Primary School

Feelings

Love is red like red, red rubies
It looks like the centre of a heart
It feels like a jewel in my hands
It smells like chocolate, smothered over my face
It sounds like a beating pulse
It tastes like the beauty of love on my tongue
It reminds me of red roses glistening in the rain.

Jodie Penketh (9)
Bleak Hill Primary School

Feelings

Sadness is red like a broken heart
It sounds like a person banging on a table
It looks like a pool of tears
It tastes like a bowl of something stale
It smells like a burning fire
It feels like grains of sand slipping out of my hands
It reminds me of something sad.

Charlotte Polding (9)
Bleak Hill Primary School

Feelings

Anger is orange like the burning sun
It feels like a knife being stabbed inside you
It smells like wood in a red-hot fire
It sounds like a wolf howling at a full moon
It tastes like burnt toast
It looks like a star shooting across the burning sky
It reminds me of a bonfire set alight.

Melissa Prescott (9)
Bleak Hill Primary School

Feelings

Anger is red like a hot fire
It looks like a red-hot devil
It sounds like cymbals banging
It smells like coal flaming
It tastes like toast burning
It feels like sugar crumbling
It reminds me of things smashing.

Laura Ramsay (10)
Bleak Hill Primary School

Feelings

Love is red like rose petals falling
It feels like a soft cushion touching my face
It sounds like a waterfall falling softly
It tastes like smooth chocolate sliding down my throat
It smells like the beauty of flowers falling on my face
It looks like a star shining magically
It reminds me of a person who I used to love
But then she broke my heart!

Richard Sturgeon (10)
Bleak Hill Primary School

Feelings

Anger is blue like the darkest of nights
It smells like a dying flower in the heat of the sun
It sounds like the firing of a gun
It feels like an old worn out tyre
It looks like a knife with blood dripping from it
It tastes like stale milk
It reminds me of a glass smashing as it hits the hard ground.

Kathryn Tabern (10)
Bleak Hill Primary School

Happiness

Happiness is yellow like the morning light
Happiness sounds like the brightness of Heaven
Happiness tastes like the seas of the world
Happiness looks like the sunlight bursting through the darkness
Happiness feels like the bright green grass
Happiness smells like the clean fresh air
Happiness reminds me of the peaceful world.

Kieran Webster (10)
Bleak Hill Primary School

Feelings

Love is red like a ruby glistening
It smells like peaceful roses on a romantic night
It feels like a deep dark secret hidden in your heart
It looks like a bird flying over the pink horizon
It sounds like the crackle of the candle burning
It tastes like a chocolate heart melting in your mouth
It reminds me of the sun as it awakes at dawn.

Megan Howarth (10)
Bleak Hill Primary School

Night

To me night is a grinning girl active and running about mysteriously
Her hair is like a soft haystack, supplying food for the animals
Her clothes are like a young teacher's, sensible but stylish
She moves slowly and dreamily like walking on clouds
She speaks slowly and quiet so she doesn't wake you up
She lives in the middle of nowhere, wherever your mind takes you
Her mouth is a bible speaking only kindness
She feels like a comfy duvet washed in Lenor
Eyes, like twinkling lights on the Christmas tree.

Bethan Flynn (10)
Christ the King Catholic Primary School

Night

Night is like a silky black blanket that turns into a magical man
Night feels so warm around me
He speaks so lovingly and gentle
His hair is like natural fur
He glides over the ground and not a sound is heard
He lives in a plump and cosy bed and is comforting around me
I feel safe around Night because he is sweet and gentle.

Liam Norgate (11)
Christ the King Catholic Primary School

The Sea

The sea is powerful, great and strong
With creatures such as whales and sharks
Fish and crabs swimming day and night
But do not quake at their sight
For you're sure to give them a fright.

The wind is howling around and around
Making then a crashing sound
People in gigs will sail towards the wreck
Sailing in whirlwinds, hurting their necks
And all for the sake of wood, which the birds will peck.

While somewhere on a glorious beach
Away from the horrible leech
Where there is sand and shells
And lovely smells
Of banana and melon
I am overwhelmed.

Skigh Milne (11)
Christ the King Catholic Primary School

Night

It is coal, full of mystery and magic
From dusk till dawn is its domain
Silver shimmering stars look back from space
Mr Moon, bald-headed, fills the sky
The wispy clouds; his breath in the cold crisp air
The wind whispers as it blows through the leafless trees
The hoot of the owl like a train announcing its arrival
The darkness like a warm blanket around your body
Its comforting stillness retreating as every hour passes
Slowly creeping towards dawn
The night leaves you with a grandfatherly embrace.

Joshua Mottram (11)
Christ the King Catholic Primary School

The Sea Poem

Under the sea
There's something waiting for me
It may be silver, it may be mould, it may be cheese it may be gold
It may be great whites, which are very old.

The waves are crushing me
Most of the sea is over me
The clean sand is so sloppy
I even found a baby's nappy.

Tiger sharks are hunting for food
While fish are being rude
All the adults are smoking
While all the waves are crashing and splashing.

All the fish are swimming fast
But the sea is settling at last
A shark's fin comes to the surface
It feels like I have motion sickness
The creatures are dying
And fish are crying.

Andrew Toller (10)
Christ the King Catholic Primary School

Night

She is a gentle grandmother but rough as the cold sea
She is a soft new mattress but restless as a baby lion
She has a big, bold, plump, puppy-dog, daring type of eyes
Her small, smirky, sly but always open type of mouth
Her hair is all tattered and never been brushed in her life
Her old, sweaty, dirty, ripped clothes haven't been washed
She is a bouncing, very bubbly type of trampoline
She has never in her dirty little life talked properly, she just shouts
She lives in the wild in nature with flowers
She has never sat or stood still for more than five minutes.

Jennifer Fay (11)
Christ the King Catholic Primary School

The Sea

The sea
Beside the shore
Nothing more than
The sea
Waves hitting the rocks harder
Than ever before
Nothing louder than
The sea
Mackerel, salmon, shark, shrimps
And not to mention the dolphin
That might show you a flip
The sea
The shark swam over there
The shark swam over here
If he comes near me and you
Please don't fear.

Sean McCorkindale (10)
Christ the King Catholic Primary School

Night

Night is a best friend to everyone
And she lives in the sky having jolly joyful journeys
She feels like a squishy soft pillow
And her eyes are like stars in the Milky Way
She makes me feel like a dream come true
She moves like burning hot Mars in the distance
Her clothes, as if she was an angel from outer space
Her lips dazzling like the moon
She speaks in a high dreamy voice
And her hair is a moonlit sky, blowing slowly but swiftly.

James Scott (10)
Christ the King Catholic Primary School

The Sea

Oh sea, you're in my sight
The crashing against the rocks
The storm it is whispering to me
I'm far away from the docks.

Ice cream you're in my mind
Sand so yellow and soft
Instead I'm working way beyond
And sleeping in a loft.

Thunder rumbling up above
Its powers are so bad
My crew are fighting back
So many are so sad.

All the crabs, fish and whales
Living in the sea
People telling all the tales
Of their sweethearts to be.

And so the end is near
The last anchor thrown
And everyone will say
I am the best sailor known.

Alice McCormack (10)
Christ the King Catholic Primary School

Night

She's a soft cosy blanket as big as the world
It feels like dipping in warm hot chocolate
It's like looking at pearls twinkling in the black sky
In the winter sun
Her hair is long and silky, wrapped around your body
Her clothes are simple and plain
She moves, light-footed and ghostly
Quiet and soft-toned, so gently.

Heather Randles (11)
Christ the King Catholic Primary School

Down At The Sea

Down at the sea only blue to be seen
The scales of the fish, the size of the whale
Crashes of the waves thrown against the caves
The moving of the seaweed asleep on the sand
Golden clams and those nippy crabs.

The fish having a ride as the tide goes high
Turtles turning round when coming from the sand
Starfish floating further down and the king of the sea
Has unfortunately lost his crown.

Sun shining giving the fish light
Fish being disturbed and scared away
As an occasional fish hook comes down to say hey!

Water turning round with shells coming down
Maybe from the high up grounds.

Our day has turned upside-down
Just when the anchor reached the ground
Maybe I'll see you tomorrow or the day after
So you can go home now on your boat.

Luke Rogers (11)
Christ the King Catholic Primary School

The Sea

The wind blowing in my face
People swimming and the seagulls race
Cold air, my legs are bare because of the shorts I wear
Sandcastles standing, planes are landing
Rescue boats going out to sea, birds watch gracefully.

My dad is fishing, my mum is dishing something out to eat
But the sad thing is my mum is cooking, I really can't be
bothered looking
I hear my ringtone, it's my mum, I have to go home.

Michael Arribaja (11)
Christ the King Catholic Primary School

The Sea

The sea is wonderful, powerful and strong
But when I listen to all the howling at night
I see the lighthouse and bright light
The wind is wild, tough and mad.

All types of creatures swim in the sea
Like turtles and fish full of glee
People going to coastlines on big boats
They lower their anchor with huge ropes.

The rubbish and dirt make pollution
If we recycled it could be a solution
The swish whisper of the sea
The deadly sharks horrify me.

How quiet the sea looks in the dark
What's that over there?
It could be a shark.

I listen to the sea every day
I hear the sound of the sea when I play
The sea has such a beautiful face
It reminds me of my one safe place.

Onomey Ovien (11)
Christ the King Catholic Primary School

Night

Night is a big, warm, friendly giant
Cosy, soft and comfortable all the time
And his eyes are sparkling stars
But the mouth moves like a hot sun
And the hair is a big grey moth
But the clothes are warm blankets
He moves gently like the warmth
And he speaks soft and gently
But he lives in the hot valley
And he makes me feel happy and warm.

Stephen Kelly (10)
Christ the King Catholic Primary School

Under The Sea

Under the sea
There's something for me
It's a big golden key
The swishing of the waves
There's a lot of waves
By the shire there's a big fat fish
In a dark green dish
On the bay
There's a pile of hay
And the wind doesn't stop till beautiful May
On the dolphins you're taken for a ride
In the big high tide
On the sand there's a fish and chip shop
And on the street there's a special offer for a mop
The adults are smoking
And the children are soaking
Sorry guys, that's the end of the day
We'll see you next May.

Arran Nelson (10)
Christ the King Catholic Primary School

Night

Night is warm and soft
Her eyes are pale brown
Her mouth is watering red
Her pyjamas are pink and purple stripes
She wriggles about all night
She whispers very softly
She has a big house
Night, I feel for you and care for you.

Kayleigh Woods (10)
Christ the King Catholic Primary School

The Sea

Putting up the beach tent
Putting down the picnic blanket
All of the daughters ran down to the waters
Splashing their feet to the waves' beat
Boys and girls having fun
Playing in the sand
While Mum and Dad listen to the band
Everybody having fun
In the hot sun
Looking for fish
To make the Sunday dish
Playing games
With the waves
Hunting for treasure, bronze, silver and gold
Going in the rock pool
Soaking your feet, nice and cool.

Charley Newstead (10)
Christ the King Catholic Primary School

Night

Night is as kind and loving as a grandmother
She feels soft, warm and smooth
Her eyes are like small sparkling stars
And her mouth moves very slowly
Her hair is grey, short and fluffy like a cloud
Her clothes are soft and simple
She moves elegantly and as if she is floating
She speaks gently and quietly
She lives in a small cosy cottage which looks sweet enough to eat
Night is a quiet, relaxing time.

Kate Saunders (10)
Christ the King Catholic Primary School

The Sea

The swishing of the sea
The sailing of the tourists
The soaking of the waves
The diving of the divers
The fishing of the fishermen
The sea is really fun
The sandcastles are nearly done
And today's lunch menu is a hot cross bun
The stinging of the jellyfish
The biting of the sharks
The burning of the sun
And everyone is having fun
The wrecking of the ship
The flying of the sky-diving people
The waves are soaking
And the signs says, 'No Smoking'
The smell of the picnics
How great is the sea!

Luke Hogg (10)
Christ the King Catholic Primary School

Night

He is a fiery thief lurking everywhere
He feels cold and rough like sandpaper
His eyes are like coal and forever dead
His mouth is like a deep well, black and terrifying
His clothes like a dark pool of dirt but mysterious
He moves as if he was a cat himself, slick and sly
He will speak but not much is heard so quiet and low
He lives in an alleyway with the darkness of the sky
He will make you feel as if you are so cold
You're frozen and you will always get the shivers and be frightened.

Elizabeth Fletcher (10)
Christ the King Catholic Primary School

The Sea Poem

In the seas there's something for me
A banana boat and waves covering the sea
A weird fish that looks like a bee
Even a fruit like kiwi is under the sea
But don't forget it can be dangerous
With the poisonous fish that can be contagious.

Ice cream, chippy buns and doughnuts
All the nice food you'll have at the sea
Fish and chips you'll have to eat
And your mum might get you a treat.

Under the sea there's a shipwreck
And if you're lucky
There'll be treasure
If you want a tan
Then lay on the sand because the sun is so bright
The kids fly a kite
And the sharks want to fight
That's the end of the day
We will see you next May.

Connor Toolan (10)
Christ the King Catholic Primary School

Night-Time

Night is a shiny star in the moonlit sky
A cosy grandmother, warm and hot
Night is white and shiny like Heaven
Speaks so softly like a rainy cloud
Night has hair, blonde as twinkly stars
Night is calm, jolly and happy
Night lives in a place like Heaven but in a nice cosy cottage
Night, I like so much
Night is lovely, warm and cosy
Oh Night, what would I do without thee?

Jack Peters (10)
Christ the King Catholic Primary School

The Sea

Making a sandcastle on a hot summer day
Eating an ice cream with its lovely dairy way
Wind howling, whooshing through your hair
People fishing in the sea
Shark's in the water looking for his tea
Fish talking to one another
Big rocks what kids stand on
And I am queen of the world
So grant me a glass of water.

White horses rolling over
Coming towards you and soaking your feet
Seagulls going lower and lower to the sea
Using beaks to find something to eat
People diving and going to the bottom of the sea
Finding treasure to share with one another.

Natasha Woods (10)
Christ the King Catholic Primary School

Night

His hair is thick among the misty moons
Eyes are beady looking through dizzy visions
He hardly says a word as he walks through the galaxies
Feels comfortable but senses danger
He is slow and grazed
Hair which is crying for help
He is as fat as an elephant
As the deep, dark danger
Mouth covered with white wrinkles
Wears clothes smelly, dirty and sweaty
Does not make a sound
And yet cannot get to sleep.

Daniel Redmond (10)
Christ the King Catholic Primary School

The Sea

In the sea there's a big shiny key
Divers go under the sea
To fetch the big shiny key
The waves cover the sea so I go in the water
And then I see my grandaughter
Even fruit like kiwi
Is under the deep blue sea
Under the sea is a shipwreck
And a person called Shrek
Seagulls flying round for ice cream
And little kids have sun cream
In the sea there's people swimming around
And people wandering around.

Fish and chips you will have to eat
And then your mum will give you a treat
If they want a tan
They will lay in the sand
Because the sun is so bright
There's kids flying a kite
There are sharks trying to bite
This is the end of the day
We will see you next May.

Jack Kemp (11)
Christ the King Catholic Primary School

Sleep

Sleep is a warm chatty grandmother
It is always baking something that smells delicious
Sleep lives in a warm cosy house with a fire always lit
Crackling leaves being stepped on
Sleep is always ready for a warm hug
Sleep wears an apron that's always covered in flour
Sleep's eyes are warm and comforting
Sleep always wears reading glasses
Sleep speaks slowly and calmly.

Callum Grant (11)
Christ the King Catholic Primary School

Night

She is a gentle caring grandmother
She shines so brightly like a red colourful ruby
She feels like a warm, plump sunny day
And a bright morning on a sandy beach
Her eyes are sparkling like a dazzling fish
Her mouth is bright shining red like the sunset on a clear day
Her hair is curly and grey like frosty cold ice
Her clothes are smooth and ironed and the colour of a clear blue pool
She moves silently through the bright moonlight
She speaks soft and caringly
She lives in a warm, cosy cottage in the middle of the
bright green countryside.

Daniel Ward (11)
Christ the King Catholic Primary School

Night Is . . .

A soft cosy giant lighting a fire
His eyes are as bright as brass buttons
He is king of darkness and sleep
His nose is a crescent moon
With hands that are gentle and soft
Holding me like a baby
His feet stand across hills and valleys
With legs as long as the tallest trees
And as black as soot
He hides behind my curtains
And glides like a swan, quiet and calm
I welcome Night because he brings me peace and rest.

Aidan Piercy (11)
Christ the King Catholic Primary School

The Sea Poem

The sea is blue, a bit green
The waves can be a little mean
The sea is loud
Floats above sandy ground.

When the moon is out at night
The sea becomes a floating light
The sea gently floats through the day
So the children can come and play.

The sea can swish and swoosh
Also wash and whoosh
The sea is great for an ice cream
To wish and dream.

Chloe Walsh (10)
Christ the King Catholic Primary School

Night

He is a jumping-jack
He is a calm, small sweet night
He is as soft as a just-washed duvet
His eyes are small stars lighting up the sky
His mouth is big as the Milky Way
His clothes, so warm as he cuddles up
His hair, so soft like silk
His voice, so calm
He lives like a small cottage in the woods
He is like a spring morning
I love him so much
He is my baby cousin.

Abbie Harvey (11)
Christ the King Catholic Primary School

The Sea

The animals at the sea are great
Fishing with my fishing bait
Children on the banana boat
And swimming in their little moat
People buying souvenirs
Like bumper stickers for car rears
Lugworms in the wet sand
Around the guitarist in the band
Crabs crawling sideways
Incoming my ways
Jellyfish floating in the sea
I really hope they don't sting me
Eating sardines on the beach
Had a swim and caught a leech
Far away I see a whale
Now there is a terrible gale
Teenagers having a surf
Children watching Grandma Smurf
In the horizon there is a typhoon
To swim out there you are a fool
Picking up lots of shells
Now what's that stink, it really smells
Over there is a fish
Good enough for a king's dish
Over there is a whale
I think it is a female
If you go on holiday, why not make a reach
For our very local beach!

Alex Dwyer (11)
Christ the King Catholic Primary School

The Sea

Under the sea, under the sea
Under the sea, under the sea
It's getting better
It's getting wetter just for me
Poseidon is ruling
Crabs are snoozing
Under the sea.

Under the sea, under the sea
Under the sea, under the sea
The waves are crashing
The wind is bashing only for he
It's now a new day
The fish are going to break away
Under the sea.

Under the sea, under the sea
Under the sea, under the sea
The pebbles are lying
Great whites are dying
It's getting big, the tide
The fish are going to hide
Or the sharks will eat them alive
Under the sea.

Under the sea, under the sea
Under the sea, under the sea
Wrecks are lying
Seagulls are flying under the sea
The tide is low
The whales are eating Pinocchio
Under the sea.

Joseph McCorkindale (10)
Christ the King Catholic Primary School

The Sea

The animals in the sea are great
That's why I just can't wait
The sea is very choppy
My ice cream is very sloppy
A big whale and a sea snail
An amazingly huge crab
Whilst eating a massive kebab
The sea is really fun
The sand sculptures are done
People just adore
The sea has more and more
Of great things to do
For people like me and you
I would love to have a dish
Of a piece of fabulous fish
The sea is next to sand
Where people can get tanned
That's why I can't wait
To get my fishing bait
Kids as young as three
Can still play in the sea
I want to get my boat
And sail around the moat
We go on holiday
Just to get away
From our homes
And all those moans and groans
If you don't love the sea now
It is hard to know how!

Stephen Smith (11)
Christ the King Catholic Primary School

The Sea

Under the sea
There is something waiting for me
It may be silver, it may be gold
But in the sea it is very cold.

Inside an old shipwreck
Was hiding a big green Shrek
Then the shipwreck got washed up
Then some friends found an ancient cup.

On a sunny day on the sea
Some people had a kiwi
When the sea gets a high tide
Some people take a jet boat for a ride.

When the waves wee going out
All the children gave a shout
All the adults were smoking
When the children were soaking.

All the adults were having food
When the children were in a jolly mood
An adult was looking for a shell
When he saw a lovely girl called Mel.

When we looked at the big shiny sun
Everyone remembered what fun they had had
This is the end of the day
So we'll see you next May.

Tom Kemp (11)
Christ the King Catholic Primary School

Under The Sea

Under the sea there is something for me
Like my old friend Tom P
There are fish
They don't eat food on the dish.

Under the sea there is a great white shark
It does not bark
People ride jet boats
And they wear wet coats.

Under the sea there is a boat
That didn't float
They're dangerous things
Not like wings.

Under the sea there are shells
Those don't ring like bells
In low tide
People are more kind

So now you know about the sea
Why don't you ride down?

Tom Lowry (10)
Christ the King Catholic Primary School

The Sea

The sea is great for you and for me
The creatures that live
Eating people for tea.

The ice creams excite
With an eye after eye
And when I look over, a big cream pie.

There are sailors, divers and fishermen too
There's lighthouses looking around for you.

Thomas Parkinson (10)
Christ the King Catholic Primary School

The Sea

The sea
Is fantastic
All the fish swimming in the sea gracefully
Through the sea
All the children building sandcastles
And boats going out to sea
And ferries with lots of people going on holiday
The boats coming back with lots of fish
And all the people have left and the sea is quiet once again.

Andrew Jones (11)
Christ the King Catholic Primary School

Mr Mass Who Ate Some Grass

There was a man called Mr Mass
Who always loved to eat some grass
Then one day he had wobbly knees
Because he had caught a dreadful disease
He turned into a big brown cow
I really do not know how.

The following day his hooves turned to jelly
And he sprouted blue hairs all over his belly
Mr Mass thought he should stop eating grass
Until his dreadful symptoms would pass.

Harrison Royds (8)
Farnborough Road Junior School

Dog - Haiku

The dog ran quickly
Up my bedroom, down the stairs
Dog, cat, not good friends.

Elizabeth Fitzpatrick (11)
Farnborough Road Junior School

The Desolate City

The city lay dead
Gasping in endless, but staggered breaths of stale night air
Buildings stood crouched, bleeding whilst seeming listless and dilapidated
Streets were desolate and uninspiring
A lighted cigarette roamed aimlessly before being seen off
By a miserable empty bottle attempting to keep law and order
The cigarette took offence as it ignited the bottle
The bottle screeched in helplessness
As the cigarette fled at lightning speed in the other direction
Acting like a deadly inferno fed by wooden housing beams and car fuel
Converting everything into charcoal
The fire now teetered over a cliff of self-exterminating acid
But then it fell over the edge - oblivious to its surroundings
And ignoring the screams of its victims
The blaze became so hot, that it consumed itself
This was the city's finest hour!

Nick Lawson (11)
Farnborough Road Junior School

The Volcano

As the calm, silent volcano stood in his place on the land
All of a sudden a colossal amount of red-hot lava burst out
of his spiky spout and cried
He howled mercilessly
As hard mean rocks and gigantic pieces of burning stone
Grazed his inside skin as they tried to escape his mean horrible body
The angry volcano calmed down and slowly stopped feeding
the ground with lava.

Lucy Wright (10)
Farnborough Road Junior School

Hurricane

The colossal hurricane wraps its arms around many screaming people
It spins them round and round and finally throws them
onto the stony streets of America
People and houses shout for help but the hurricane ignores
Running backwards and forwards
The hurricane drags more innocent people by the throats
and spins furiously
Then it carries them up and up . . .
And laughs a high cruel laugh and drops them from a huge height
Bang! They hit the ground
The hurricane laughs more and more as people run forward
to see their loved ones
It goes round to people's houses and knocks on the brown
wooden doors
Crashing houses down, then finally the hurricane disappears
and no more is heard!

Ellis Watkinson (11)
Farnborough Road Junior School

Furious Flood

The floodwaters move in on the small town of New Orleans
Seizing the town by the throat and engulfing it in water
Quickly it wraps itself around a small cottage and crushes it
For it has seen a large flat
It crawls through an open window
Into an apartment belonging to a young mother and child
The girl screams, but it's too late
The water has already grabbed her lungs
After claiming its first victim
It moves on to the whole town
Then devouring the whole village
It slinks off like a snake to the next unwilling *city!*

Lauren Urquhart (11)
Farnborough Road Junior School

The Writer Of This Poem . . .

(Inspired by 'The Writer of this Poem' by Roger McGough)

Is as slow as a snail
As strong of a hammer
As gentle as a fingernail.

As fast as a car
As slow as a turtle
As happy as a star
As silly as moaning Myrtle

As dumb as a bat
As good as gold
As woolly as a hat
Is strong and bold.

Daniel Holden (9)
Farnborough Road Junior School

A Brown Monkey

Jungle jumper
Nut eater
High swinger
Noise maker
Banana lover
Branch climber
A brown monkey.

Emma Vizard (11)
Farnborough Road Junior School

Dragon - Haiku

Fire dragon at night
With powerful sapphire wings
And great crystal claws.

Charles Lavelle (10)
Farnborough Road Junior School

My Fun Day

My fun day
Starts with a bang
I get out of bed
Trip up and shout, *'Dang!'*

We go and have breakfast
It's toast and porridge today
My mum tells me to go to school
I shout, *'No way!'*

Besides shouting
I get dressed
I go to school
And do my best.

Rhys Storer (9)
Farnborough Road Junior School

Thunder Woe

Thunder wonder
Hitting the ground
Making holes
All around
Pounding
And rebounding off
The world
Turning
It into
A miserable
Town.

Callum Whitehead (10)
Farnborough Road Junior School

Lion

Maned racer
Zebra chaser
Huge prowler
Great growler
People scarer
Mane wearer
Fab roarer
African tourer
Big cat
Take that.

Ruth Jones (10)
Farnborough Road Junior School

Kennings - Dogs

Fast runner
Ball lover
Bone eater
Cat beater
Grass digger
Mutley snigger

What am I?
A: A dog!

Lydia Rylance (11)
Farnborough Road Junior School

Lemonade

Lemonade is very fizzy
Sometimes it makes you dizzy
It bubbles and bubbles up and up
Till it gets to the top of the cup.

Charlotte Wrigg (8)
Farnborough Road Junior School

If I Were . . .

If I were a mermaid . . .
I could let my hair go free
Flipping my tail gracefully
Gliding in the coral reef
With a shimmering tail
I could swim in the most elegant way
Dancing around the dolphins
Chasing the sharks away
Happily swimming with the fish
I would sit on the rocks out of the bay
I'd sparkle in the sunlight
I would splash up and down
Without a care in the world
I'd be in a world in the sea
If only I were a mermaid.

Emma Grant (9)
Farnborough Road Junior School

The Writer Of This Poem

(Inspired by 'The Writer of this Poem' by Roger McGough)

The writer of this poem is . . .
Bigger than a plane
As strong as a book
As gentle as a mane

As fast as a cheetah
As slow as a mouse
As happy as a big eater
As silly as a house

As small as a chair
As slow as a snail
As big as a bear
And is faster than a gale.

Jessica Dale (9)
Farnborough Road Junior School

The Christmas Poem

C hristmas tree all night long
H appy singers sing a song
R inging bells from the reindeer I hear
I ce will give you chills I fear
S now on Santa
T ree with Prancer
M ince pies for people
A ngels all around
S leigh on the ground.

Adam Gregson (10)
Farnborough Road Junior School

The Earthquake

The Earth shakes with malicious laughter
The world shivers in shock thereafter
The whole of the world appeared awake
As waters ripple and countries quake
Lights are switched on in houses and streets
The heart of the world takes faster beats
The world stops and goes back to sleep
The countries and waters make no peep.

Alexandra Knight (10)
Farnborough Road Junior School

Where Do Fairies Come From?

Where do fairies come from?
You really want to know
And are they very tiny or do they sometimes grow?
There are many types of fairies and most you will never see
They hide in secret places like a plant, nest or tree
In the secret world of fairies you will have a special treat
Because some very special fairies are here for you to meet!

Amy Burrows (10)
Farnborough Road Junior School

What Is The Sun?

The sun is like a red gluestick lid sitting in a blue pencil case
It is like a big yellow flower placed in a clear blue vase
It is like a juicy yellow melon dropped on a blue tablecloth
It is like a goldfish being washed up by the blue sea
It is like an amber jewel sat in a blue casket
It is like a golden plate put on a blue tablecloth
It is like a yellow pin stick into a light blue notice board
It is like a piece of pineapple on a blue plate.

Vandolyn Oldham (10)
Farnborough Road Junior School

If I Were . . .

If I were a lion . . .
My roar would make mountains crumble
My mane would shake powerfully in the wind
I could prance and dance in the jungle
I could catch loads of prey in one hunt
I could scare the most fearless animals
All animals would be honoured just to see me.

Lucy Wright (9)
Farnborough Road Junior School

If I Were . . .

If I was a lion in ancient Roman times . . .
I would curl up in my dark gloomy cage
Then in the morning I would get whipped into the Coliseum
Then snarl around and leap on the helpless victim ripping him limb from limb
Then fight the other animals over the flesh.

James Wall (9)
Farnborough Road Junior School

What Am I?

Love
Warm hug
Tea mug
Sweet kiss
Sometimes miss
Having fun
In the sun
It is an emotion
What am I?
Love!

Aaron Mawdsley-Welsh (10)
Farnborough Road Junior School

If I Were . . .

If I were a bird . . .
I would swoop from tree to tree
I would sing very happily with people feeding me
I'd build a beautiful nest
I'd curl up tight
I'd whisper to my babies,
'Ssssshh, goodnight!'

Chantelle Doherty (10)
Farnborough Road Junior School

If I Were . . .

If I were a lion . . .
I could roar as loud as could be
I could sprint through the jungle hitting leaves and vines
My mane would glisten in the sunshine as I stand on a rock
I would be the proudest animal
If only I were a lion.

David Johnson (9)
Farnborough Road Junior School

Shark Attack

Shark!
With the two eyes like black holes
Its terrifying grin would make your stomach turn
As its streamlined body swivels towards you
Almost like an acrobat
Its fins like knives
It was as long as a yacht
And its teeth like razors
You wouldn't want to come across
A shark!

James Sutton (10)
Farnborough Road Junior School

What Am I?

Maybe round
Sometimes sound
Maybe square
Always aware
Tells time
Can chime
Under sleeve
Never leave!

Luke Williams (10)
Farnborough Road Junior School

If I Were . . .

If I were a butterfly . . .
I'd escape into the wild
I'd search for insects to gobble up for tea
And find a place to hibernate, to snuggle up for winter
And once I'd woken up I'd swing and sway till I found my way!

Molly Jameson (9)
Farnborough Road Junior School

Hello Dragon

Hello dragon with the emerald scales
Hello dragon with the extremely long nails
Hello dragon, are you the only one?
I'm the dragon, yes I am the only one
Hello dragon, what fiery breath
Hello dragon, you will never know death.

Hello dragon, what a long curly horn
Hello dragon, your prey will come at dawn
Hello dragon, we never see you pass by
Hello dragon, swooping through the sky
Hello dragon, sharpening your claws
Hello dragon, opening your wide jaws.

Hello dragon, flying as well as a bee
Hello dragon, *it's coming to eat me!*

Lucy Day (10)
Farnborough Road Junior School

What Is The Sun?

The sun is a crispy golden leaf floating on a clear glowing stream
It is a golden eagle flying through a pale blue door towards Heaven
It is an illuminated pumpkin sitting by a glittering blue river
It is a golden diamond sitting on a flowing turquoise cloth
It is a fiery ray gliding through the pearly-blue sea.

Kathryn Yates (10)
Farnborough Road Junior School

What Is The Sun?

The sun is a yellow flower put in a blue vase
It is a yellow snake curled up into a ball on top of a blue wall
It is an orange windmill in a blue pot filled with soil
It is a round orange ice cream melting on a blue table.

Jonathan Lydiate (9)
Farnborough Road Junior School

If I Were . . .

If I were a hummingbird . . .
I would sing the sweetest songs
I'd flap my wings gracefully gliding over the most beautiful landscapes
I'd feel the wind beating in my face
I'd fly to the most exotic islands eating the rarest fruits
Soaring over the oceans letting my feet feel the warmth of the sea
I'd make my nest up in the greenest tree watching the flowers bloom
I'd hunt for food on the brightest summer day
I'd watch the humans sing and dance under a dark moonlit sky
I'd mate and have children who would carry on my role.

Rory Crowther (10)
Farnborough Road Junior School

What Is The Sun?

The sun is a sandbank in the middle of the deep blue ocean
It is a lemon clock generating power on a pale blue wall
It is the yellow feathers flickering on a blue tit's breast
It is a golden lion keeping guard at water's edge
It is a gleaming piece of topaz shining on a sapphire cushion
It is a flash of sheet lightning reflecting against the shimmering waters
It is a glistening pearl resting in a purple oyster's mouth.

Oliver Adams (9)
Farnborough Road Junior School

What is The Sun?

The sun is a ginger cat curling up in its little blue basket
The sun is an orange tablet staring at me in its pale blue jar
It's like a tempting yellow lemon lying on the beautiful rocky river
It's like a tri-coloured ball standing on a light blue skyscraper
It's like an orange basketball shooting for its small blue hoop
It's like a yellow smiley face sticker, sticking on a dark blue jumper.

Jack Young (10)
Farnborough Road Junior School

World War III

I think there's going to be
A rather unpleasant World War III
When aliens will invade the Earth
And bend over double shrieking with mirth
At our foolish attempts to achieve our goal
Getting those aliens to do what they're told.

I think there's going to be
A rather gruesome World War III
When creepy-crawlies
Will make us all poorly
We will need to get
A giant net
And if they still lurk
I don't know what will work!

Emma Taggart (10)
Farnborough Road Junior School

The Writer Of This Poem Is . . .

(Inspired by 'The Writer of this Poem' by Roger McGough)

As arty as a smarty
As clever as a fox
As happy as a bee
As strong as a box

As fluffy as a cloud
As funny as a bunny
As pretty as a flower
As good as money

As helpful as my sister
As cute as a bear
As delightful as Miss Jones
As fun as a fair

The writer of this poem is me!

Jade Townsend (9)
Farnborough Road Junior School

Potion Magic

(Inspired by 'Macbeth')

Start this potion, make it bubble
Deliver sadness, evil and trouble
Donkey's hoof and lion's mane
Cry of a slaughtered warthog's pain
Dragon's horn and bluebottle wings
Give me the essence of a reeking king

Add a cat's ear and petals of rose
Flatten the point of an elephant nose
Take two twigs from beaver's dam
Throw in a gold pearl of angry clam
As soon as the full moon comes into sight
Collect the outside shine of light

Vampire's cape, Devil's hair
Ten tiny stones from the honey bear's lair
Nettle sting - makes it sharp
Bendy string from golden harp
Mouldy earwax, cow dung
Claw of newt and camel's lung
Stripe of tiger all long and black
Feather of a budgie and duckling's quack
Small slimy slugs, slip them in
Misty monkey eyes make them spin
As the stormy clouds appear
Catch a raindrop from far and near.

This wicked potion is coming to an end
Soon Macbeth to Hell we'll send
All together, one, two, three
Let us chant and you will see
How it burns, how it boils
Now Macbeth is in our coils!

Freyja Erickson-Rohrer (11)
Farnborough Road Junior School

Mermaid Girl

The carved wooden comb went through her long locks
of golden strands
Glistening in the shimmering of the enchanted moonlight's
radiant beams
Her face is freshly fallen snow, white and dainty against her
blood-red lips
Eyes are blue sapphires, shimmering against her bare skin
Song of an angel, it is a young mother's lullaby
But deadly, sailors bow down to her beauty

A crack of thunder, whirlwinds, lagoons angry at her presence!
Then silent, as if nothing had occurred that night
Except for a chestnut-coloured comb, bobbing along in the sea . . .

Holly Fletcher (10)
Farnborough Road Junior School

What Is The Sun?

The sun is a red apple rising over a quiet blue sea
It is an orange racing car driving over a black-tinted motorway
It is a red sunflower swaying on a blue field
It is a red football kicked into a summer sky
It is a golden pound found rolling on a yellow table
The sun is a lonely star in space.

Max Noble (10)
Farnborough Road Junior School

If I Were A Monkey . . .

If I were a monkey . . .
I would swing from vine to vine eating nuts and bananas
I would show off in front of all my monkey friends shouting all the way
Only if I were a monkey.

Bethan Bowden (9)
Farnborough Road Junior School

If I Were . . .

If I were a horse . . .
I would charge through the valley
I would graze among the haystacks
I would trot up the cobbled streets and leave behind hoof tracks
I would chase my brown hairy tail
I would rear up at the butterflies and neigh at the rooster
who just let out his wail
I would rage at the annoying flies
If I were a horse I would race around the marked flags.

Lewis Cross (9)
Farnborough Road Junior School

What Is The Sun?

The sun is a yellow flower growing in a blue vase
It is a golden plate standing on a blue table
It is a tangy mango sitting in a blue fruit bowl
It is an amber jewel gleaming in a blue casket
It is a melting ice cream laying in a blue cone
It is a flame being put out by blue water
It is a yellow bird flying by a light blue plane
It is a golden ring shining in a blue box.

Tilly Walters (10)
Farnborough Road Junior School

What Is The Sun?

The sun is like a golden eagle shining down to the wonderful
blue Earth
It's red like a fire engine and yellow as an American taxi
It is shining in the dark black space with Neptune
Showing it's wonderful planet of blue
It is a red apple shooting into the sky
It's a yellow literacy folder in 51 classroom sitting on a black shelf.

Aimée Ferreira (9)
Farnborough Road Junior School

If I Were . . .

If I were a cheetah . . .
I'd run so far
I'd run so fierce
I'd feel the wind in my face
Every time I would run
I'd be the fastest ever
I'd be top of the food chain
No one would catch me
I can imagine it now
Just as if I were a cheetah.

Ananga Campbell (9)
Farnborough Road Junior School

What Is The Sun?

The sun is like a red bus driving along tarmac
It is a juicy strawberry falling from a dark bush
It is like an orange squirting from the black sky
It is a banana in a monkey's home
It is like an eagle floating through the summer sky
It is a yellow submarine rushing through the sea.

Robson Baldwin (10)
Farnborough Road Junior School

What Is The Sun?

The sun is like a red bus driving along tarmac
It is like strawberries being eaten under a blue sky
It is like fire coming from a black dragon's mouth
It is like a yellow T-shirt put against a black ball gown
It is like bright bold flowers standing next to blue violets
It is like yellow literacy books next to blue numeracy books.

Chloe Burrill (9)
Farnborough Road Junior School

If I Were A . . .

If I were an elephant . . .
I'd swing my trunk around
I'd stamp on people with my big feet (if I wanted to)
I'd live in the most beautiful places like Africa and Asia
I'd get my food with my trunk and save it in my mouth
When it becomes night-time
I'll snuggle up with my friend
Ready for another day in this beautiful place.

Emma Lloyd (10)
Farnborough Road Junior School

What is The Sun?

The sun is like a yellow flower burning in fire
It is sand getting poured in blue ink
It is a gold coin dropping down into the blue sea
It is Saturn spinning around in space
It is a strawberry in a bowl of blueberries
It is a golden eagle swooping down from the midsummer sky.

Shannon Griffiths (9)
Farnborough Road Junior School

What Is The Sun?

The sun is a treasure swallowed by a black swamp
It is like a golden eagle flying through the clear blue sky
It is like a red-hot heater in the middle of endless blackness
It is a blood-red cherry growing in the blue sky
It is a fire blazing on forever in a land of burnt black wood
It is a juicy strawberry in a dark black cupboard.

Daniel Burrow (9)
Farnborough Road Junior School

About The Writer

(Inspired by 'The Writer of this Poem' by Roger McGough)

The writer of this poem
Is as shiny as a key
As strong as a metal door
As gentle as a bee

As fast as a tick
As slow as a snail
As happy as a little girl
As silly as a tail

As kind as a butterfly
As funny as a clown
As stupid as a zoo monkey
As sad as a little girl's frown.

Megan Taylor (8)
Farnborough Road Junior School

The Writer Of This Poem

(Inspired by 'The Writer of this Poem' by Roger McGough)

The writer of this poem
Is smaller than a bug
As strong as a wrestler
As gentle as a tug

As fast as a car
As slow as a snail
As happy as a smile
As silly as a tale

As kind as a star
As tall as a house
As good as a car
As quiet as a mouse.

Paige Fairhurst (9)
Farnborough Road Junior School

The Writer Of This Poem

(Inspired by 'The Writer of this Poem' by Roger McGough)

The writer of this poem
Is greater than a snake
As strong as a house
As gentle as a lake

As fast as a motorbike
As slow as a snail
As happy as a birthday
As silly as a whale

As happy as can be
As gentle as fluff
As slippery as slime
As lovely as a heart.

Emma Dinsdale (9)
Farnborough Road Junior School

The Writer Of This Poem

(Inspired by 'The Writer of this Poem' by Roger McGough)

The writer of this poem
Is taller than a cloud
As strong as the thickest steel
As gentle as a person who likes to sing out loud

As fast as a racing car
As slow as a snail
As happy as a star
As silly as a postman who posts all the mail

As silly as a clown
As tasty as ice cream
As grumpy as a frown
As clean as a stream.

Enna Erickson-Rohrer (9)
Farnborough Road Junior School

Animals

The snake slithers in the grass
Like a bullet slicing nothing.

The eagle sails through the air
Like a shark chasing a surfer.

The lion prowls through the jungle
Like a boy lost in a crowd.

The tiger lies in wait for prey
Like a snail sliding along in its shell.

The spider finishes making its web
Like a chef completing his delicacy.

The pig rolls in the mud
Like a sausage in the barbecue.

Alex Burgess (10)
Higher Bebington Junior School

My Mummy

My mummy was always funny
She never cared what other people thought
My mummy never cared about the money
She only needed us!

My mummy cared for us all
She washed and cleaned
But she wasn't afraid to play ball
She only needed us!

My mummy was lovely and sweet
She loved a bubbly bath
My mum loved clean sheets
She only needed us!

Zoe Lewis (10)
Higher Bebington Junior School

Big Wild Cats

I love all cats, big or small.
I love them hairy, short or tall.
The big wild cats are the best.
They are better than the rest.
My favourite is the tiger,
it has big stripes upon its back.
They are orange, white and black.
Lions come from Africa.
They are the king of the beasts.
A zebra will make a tasty feast!
Spotty cheetahs are so fast,
they are like a spell being cast!
They're the fastest mammals on the planet.
So surely nothing can catch it or can it?
I love big cats.

Kelly Cunningham (7)
Higher Bebington Junior School

Winter Morning

Winter is the king of smiles
You can see white snow for miles
All the lakes have turned to ice
And that for me is very nice
A cold, icy, frozen lake
It looks like icing on a birthday cake
All the snow starts to melt away
But now there's no snow today
Sadly the winter goes, but here comes spring
Let's see what the new season will bring.

Mathew Callanan (9)
Higher Bebington Junior School

Antarctica

The penguins at the Poles
Like pies in the fridge

The krill in the whale
Like peas in a giant

Light in the darkest gloom
Like the taunt of the angler fish

The orca in the ocean
Like a snail in its shell

The incongruous shark, white
As the palest cream

The parrot fish chewing on coral
Like dogs chewing on a bone

The dogfish in its purse
Like caviar in a bottle

The guillemots and razor-bills in the cliff face
Like maggots on a corpse

Summer in its last hours
Like a crow's caw, loud and harsh

The polar bear in its domain
Like the grey on the elephant

Cubs, silvery and fluffy frolicking about
Like lambs in the meadows

The stranded moose on the ice shelves
Like a fish out of water, helpless and feeble.

Benjamin Hughes (11)
Higher Bebington Junior School

I Wish

Do you ever wish for one million things a day?
But it never really happens that way.

I wish I was a star but it never really happens
My brother wishes for a bar but it never really happens
I wish I could fly a million miles high but it never really happens
My mum wishes to bake the perfect pie but it never really happens

I don't understand why it doesn't I wonder
I guess it never really happens.

Talia Laing (11)
Higher Bebington Junior School

Winter Morning

Winter is a giant polar bear
Turning green fields into a funfair
Snow is falling on all the grey slates
As I run along as I am very late
Outside it is snowing
It feels like the world is glowing
All the lakes have transformed into ice
And that for me is very nice.

Carrie Chapman (9)
Higher Bebington Junior School

Time

As time goes by
I always think time flies
I hear a tick-tock
To my surprise it's a clock
I love it when school ends
I always play with my friends
Do you like time?
Well ha, time is all mine.

Tash Evans (9)
Higher Bebington Junior School

New Look

I walked into New Look and the lady said to me,
'It's a better deal now, 'cause it's buy one get one free.'
Wow! Those combats look nice
And they're at a very low price
That dress is a very pretty blue
And it is stylish too!
That scarf is fluffy and pink
It would keep me warm on the ice rink
Those flip-flops have gorgeous yellow beads
The bottom of them has a pattern like reeds.
When I bought all my things I went home
Ran upstairs and picked up my phone.
Called my friend Madeline Muck
And she went straight over to New Look.

Jessica George & Sophie McEntee-Morris (11)
Higher Bebington Junior School

Silver

Slowly, silently drifts the moon
Sparkling the night in her shining gloom.

She wakes to guard the dark night
Sprinkling silver drops of light.

Diamond dewdrops glistening on the floor
She appears to brighten up the hinges of the door

A shining cobweb glistening brightly
The silver moon dancing lightly.

She creeps across the glistening sky
She watches people say goodbye.

Alex Money (10)
Higher Bebington Junior School

The Happy And The Sad

Freezing dusk is ending
Like a slow trap of despair
Sadness is around the place
Here and everywhere
But the snake is slithering a dance
Like when a disco's in full swing
And the pandas are all so content
Like a royal majestic king
A tropical butterfly has just been formed
Like a rainbow glowing into life

Sadness is creeping in the shadows
Like a spy on a secret mission
Trying to catch many innocent people
Into its shady grasp
But the endangered tigers are sleeping peacefully
Like a baby in a cot
The African elephants just plod on
Like soldiers on patrol
And the penguins swim rapidly through the sea
Like a torpedo searching for a target

Sadness tries to overcome misery
Yet happiness is always around
So keep on the bright side
Keep your smile on.

George Anderson & William Throssell (11)
Higher Bebington Junior School

Computer Mice

Can anyone give me advice
About what to do with computer mice?
At night they come out
And race all about
Each mouse and its spouse
Invading my house
They wreck my office
And they're not too nice
What to do with computer mice?
Wait, I hadn't thought about that -
Perhaps I'll get a computer cat!

Harry Wilson & Jamie Shorrock (11)
Higher Bebington Junior School

Wintertime

Winter is the king of breeze
As it lands on the ground, starts to freeze
All the shiny lakes have turned to ice
And that for me is very nice
All the people are enjoying rosé wine
And they all think it's so divine
All the snow starts to melt away
But look some sunny sunshine is coming today.

Alexander McDermott (9)
Higher Bebington Junior School

Tim Cahill

Great boxer
Hard man
Net breaker
Number seventeen
Australian legend.

Warren Kirkby (9)
Holy Name RC Primary School

Sunny Spring Days

All of the chicks as fluffy as clouds
All of the animals are so loud

The sun dances through the sky
And rapidly the birds fly

New life is throughout the land
April showers fall gently and

Flowers share their lovely scent
Spring has come, but now it's went!

Emma Cowell (11)
Holy Name RC Primary School

The Mad Mazy Moon

I dance across the dark blue sky
Sometimes I ask myself why?
People down below are asleep
So I glide and don't make a peep.
Twinkling stars shine away
As my light fades away.
I go around the world in just one night
And I also bring my light.

Rosie Hunter (11)
Holy Name RC Primary School

The Wolf

Loud howler
Meat ripper
Sneaky runner
Cute face
Long whiskers.

Antonia Hamer (8)
Holy Name RC Primary School

Kittens!

Sipping water
Small paws
Fluffy fur
Wet nose
Little tail.

Abbie-Lee Rendell (9)
Holy Name RC Primary School

My Friend

Special person
Kind listener
Comforting pillow
Never down
Other half.

Chloe English (9)
Holy Name RC Primary School

My Baby

Sleepy head
Big crier
Messy thing
Food biter.

Rebecca Gore (9)
Holy Name RC Primary School

A Little Puppy - Haiku

Little brown puppy
Sitting on a window sill
Not a peep of noise.

Rhiannon Beacon (9)
Holy Name RC Primary School

Bug Chant

Small bugs, grow bugs
Find it hard to go bugs.

Small bugs, tall bugs
Find them in a hall bugs.

Tanned bugs, sand bugs
Find them on your hand bugs.

Kind bugs, timed bugs
Very hard to find bugs.

Ground bugs, sound bugs
Never found a pound bugs.

Katie Redmond (9)
Holy Name RC Primary School

Lion

Fierce fighter
Mean creature
Human eater
Golden fur
Super growler.

Christy McHale (9)
Holy Name RC Primary School

My Puppy

Cat chaser
Puppy racer
Cheeky monkey
Meat eater
Home lover.

Jessica Jones (9)
Holy Name RC Primary School

A Day In Summer

On the first day of summer's eve,
On the oldest tree grew the youngest leaf.
In the sky, on that beautiful day,
The happiest sun came out to play.

'Here come the clouds! Not fair, go away!'
Yelled the sun in an explosive rage,
That was the day that Elle discovered sage.

Out danced the sun, in skipped the clouds,
All day this continued, around and around.
Along came the wind and Elle heard him say,
'Here I come, hip hip hooray!'

He blew away the clouds, the day became lovely,
Then the river gurgled, moreover, became bubbly,
As bubbly as a bath, nice and warm for Mr Grundy.

Emma Walsh (11)
Holy Name RC Primary School

What Is Snow?

Snow is a pillow breaking into feathers
Snow is a balloon coming down to the ground
Snow is a sheet tucking up the ground into a deep sleep
Snow is a flake coming off the trees
Snow is a feather coming off a bird.

Liam Cooper (9)
Holy Name RC Primary School

What Is . . . Snow?

Snow is nature's carpet placed gently on the ground
It is cotton wool floating down from the sky
Snow is white balloons floating down from the clouds
Snow is a giant ice cream dropped upon the ground.

Bethany Lyons (9)
Holy Name RC Primary School

The Wonderful Waves Of The Sea

The waves of the sea, dance with great gladness
The waves of the sea, splash with sadness.

The waves of the sea, shine in the moonlight
The waves of the sea, shout for the shiny sunlight.

The waves of the sea, jump like a rabbit
The waves of the sea, make it a horrible habit.

The waves of the sea, make you dream
The waves of the sea, is not how it seems.

The waves of the sea, have a free life in the sea
This is of course the lovely life of the sea.

Rinju Philip (11)
Holy Name RC Primary School

Clouds

Clouds are beautiful cotton buds stuck on pale blue pieces of paper
They are soft fragile feathers floating on a misty sea
They are lost aeroplanes from the Bermuda Triangle infested
with white moths
Clouds are big enormous pieces of white candyfloss not even
giraffes can reach.

Milan Naji (10)
Holy Name RC Primary School

Clouds Are . . .

Balls of cotton wool blown up into the sky
Sheep walking around on pale blue paper
Feathers out of a giant's pillow being tossed up into the air
Fluff balls being sucked up by a giant's Hoover
White sheets up in the sky.

Maisie Hargreaves (10)
Holy Name RC Primary School

The Big Blanket That Covers The Road

Sometimes slowly, sometimes quickly
But always very soft.

Each flake different
Each flake white.

I cover the floor like a blanket
I also bring lots of delight.

Roll in me, make a snow angel
Or even make a snowman
And the best one of all
Is having a snowball fight.

And always remember when I disappear
I will be back again with more delight.

Amy Sawtell (10)
Holy Name RC Primary School

Clouds Are . . .

Feathers from a dove floating in the air
The white fluffy pieces of cotton being stuck on a big blue piece
of paper
A flock of sheep swimming in a large puddle of water
Pillows being thrown in an Everton bedroom and then ready
to be slept on.

Daniel Wharton (10)
Holy Name RC Primary School

What Is A . . . Cloud?

A cloud is a white pillow placed on a blue blanket
It is a ball of cotton wool, soft and cuddly
It is a sheep's fur, white and fluffy
It is candyfloss twirling around in the candyfloss machine.

Jessica Gilchrist (10)
Holy Name RC Primary School

The Shimmering Sun

The beautiful bright sun is a piece of gold
It dances in and out of the emerald hilltops
The sun glows brighter than a light
And is as beautiful as a newborn baby
As the shimmering sun dies
The hazy moon will rise and glow across us all.

Jessica Hankin (10)
Holy Name RC Primary School

Snow Is . . .

A sheet spread over the street, a bed sheet
It is nice, comfy, washed towels coming from the pale blue washing machine
A lovely, frosty, white tablecloth holding the cars as cups
Cold frosty rice pudding in a black bowl.

Jessica Doyle (10)
Holy Name RC Primary School

What Is . . . Snow?

Cotton wool rolled into a ball
White blanket lying on the floor
A cloud lay down on the ground over the grass
White tissue on the floor.

Celigreen Joy (10)
Holy Name RC Primary School

Snow Is . . .

A blanket covering the place
Is a polar bear watching the town
Millions of doves flying across the sky.

Ryan Rothwell (10)
Holy Name RC Primary School

The Bright Moon

I don't make a sound
I don't make a peep.

When people land on my back
They make a big crack.

When the rooster calls
I will go away
When I go away
I will come another day.

Adam Kinsella (10)
Holy Name RC Primary School

My Cat

Small creatures
Great teachers
Quite lazy
Doesn't go crazy
Likes fish
On its dish
Lies on a mat
It must be a cat.

Olivia Fergus (9)
Holy Name RC Primary School

The Ice

The ice is . . .
A sparkling diamond ring
A shiny window
A glass mirror laid out on to the floor
A sharp spear hanging from the floor
A clean plate falling from the sky.

Anitta Chacko (9)
Holy Name RC Primary School

The Man In The Moon

The moon is as white as lovely thick snow
He smiles at everyone he meets
And tucks them up with a goodnight kiss
And goes back up to the sky
Every time you go to bed
The moon will shine upon you.

Sara Makin (10)
Holy Name RC Primary School

Happiness

Happiness is a crimson gold
Happiness smells like sweet summer strawberries
Happiness tastes like a juicy pear
It sounds like animals running in fields
It feels like a silk dress
Happiness lives in a lavender bed
A bud of a rose, a flower's head.

Tamsin Dodd (9)
Our Lady of Pity RC Primary School

Excitement

Excitement is a light blue
It smells like a buttercup filled with love
Excitement tastes like a strawberry sponge cake
It sounds like a small breeze
It feels like you are flying
Excitement lives in your heart of hearts.

Olivia Corrigan (9)
Our Lady of Pity RC Primary School

London

A bright blue blanket waves through the sky.
Big Ben chimes to tell the nearing hour
And pierces the sky with its pointed hat.

The giant trees scratch
The cloudy sky and shadows below
The Thames flows through London
Like a long blue snake rushing through the city.

The large lamp posts climb into the trees
The silent breeze flows through the leaves.
The long railings guard the stretching Thames
Which winds and flows through London town.

Fine houses scattered around, this way and that
A line of light looks like restless fireflies swarming through the sky.

Christopher Kirby (9)
Our Lady of Pity RC Primary School

Golden Beach

The sapphire-blue sky
Is like a dolphin jumping into a lake
The golden beach
Is a lock of hair flowing in the breeze.

In the distance
There is a little midge lying under the sun
The furious waves are crashing like a mad horse.

The calm breeze
Is like a gentle hairdryer blowing against the sand
The golden waves
Are exploding into millions of colours.

Charlotte O'Hare (10)
Our Lady of Pity RC Primary School

Gloomy

Gloom is a shiny black colour
It smells like fish that has been left in the back of the fridge for years
It tastes like raw fish from the sea, not cooked.
It sounds like someone's sharpened nails running down a blackboard
It feels like an eel slipping and oozing out of your hand
Gloom lives at the bottom of the sea in people who have drowned
The burnt sienna skeletons.

Robin Coakley (9)
Our Lady of Pity RC Primary School

Happiness

Happiness is a bright yellow
It smells like the sun shining on a sunny day
Happiness tastes like joy coming into my mouth
It sounds like the sun coming down
It feels like warm air in your hands
Happiness lives inside people.

Dominic Neville (10)
Our Lady of Pity RC Primary School

Cruelty

Cruelty is red with black spots
It smells of sour milk
Cruelty tastes of sickly cheese
It sounds like wind howling
It feels like prickly thistles
Cruelty lives in a pitch-black grave.

Sam Allen (9)
Our Lady of Pity RC Primary School

At The Park

The tall trees stand high
Guarding the path below
They stand like a soldier
And they remain proudly in a row.

The top of the trees pierce the sky
That is hovering above
The sky lets out an amazing light
That spreads all over the land we love.

The thick, lush, green grass grows around the trees
Hiding the trees' growing roots
The grass lies on the ground like a gigantic green carpet
But sadly it gets flattened by boots.

Lydia Power (9)
Our Lady of Pity RC Primary School

My Autumn Walk

It was a wet and windy day
When Dad and I went on our way
The rain was coming down in sheets
Making puddles at our feet
The clouds made the sky look black, black, black.

I was glad I wore my mac, mac, mac
We went to Edinburgh Castle
Where Dad bought me a bookmark with a bright red tassel
We walked the Royal Mile, seeing things that made us smile
We were really in a rush, just in time to catch the bus
I really loved my autumn walk, where Dad and I had a great talk.

Alexandria Longworth (9)
Our Lady of Pity RC Primary School

In The Park

The trees stand tall guarding the extending path
Which is like a long, rough, grey ribbon
The grass is like a giant's hair dyed an emerald-green.

The green leaves on the tree are as smooth as a silky cloth
The bark on the tree is gritty and rough like sandpaper
The sky is as blue as a turquoise cloth draped across the top
of the trees
Its bright light glistening like a flickering candle that never goes out.

A man lies still on a dry wooden bench
Relaxing and staring into the blue sky
Hoping that the day will never end
A day of happiness and quietness.

Samantha McCauley (10)
Our Lady of Pity RC Primary School

Everlasting Hills

A man crouches down, gazing across the everlasting hills
Grinning as if it was his creation
Tho emerald-green patches of grass, dark and light.

Are also covered by a mass of tall trees and plants
The misty clouds hover slowly above the Earth
Blocking out the glistening light, bursting from the happy sun

The rocky hills and mountains are wrapped in a huge blanket
of raw green
The man takes his enchanted eyes off the everlasting landscape
And climbs down from the bumpy boulder
Smiling at the sapphire-blue river as he walks away.

Jack Haworth (10)
Our Lady of Pity RC Primary School

London

Big Ben spears up into the white pale sky
It ticks like a mouse scurrying around.

The tree stands as still as a statue in a courtyard
Its branches grab out into the air.

The river shines like a sapphire diamond with a hint of ashen
It runs like a ribbon.

A boat loiters in the water sitting on the sapphire river
Bumping into things.

Tom Gaskill (10)
Our Lady of Pity RC Primary School

The Big Ben

With amazing grace
Big Ben keeps timing and chiming along
Stands as ever in the city of London
Birds singing in the fine weather
People walking along the path by the river
A quiet and peaceful place to rest
The tree like a finger points up at the sky
The sunshine shines on the emerald-green leaves
The top of the tree spread out like an umbrella.

Ivan Li (10)
Our Lady of Pity RC Primary School

Energy

Energy is a shiny gold
That smells like fire burning in a barn
Energy tastes like smoke emerging from a racing car
That sounds like a bonfire crackling
It feels like sharp sandpaper
Energy lives in a heart of a race horse.

Megan Thomas (10)
Our Lady of Pity RC Primary School

Sunrise

The blazing sun rose in the early morning whilst I woke up
It was a fiery red colour that filled the whole sky
The sun slowly lifted itself higher and higher
Every time I opened my eyes from a blink
I rubbed my eyes in amazement
And because the light of the dazzling sun was nearly blinding me
My room was filled with sunlight
As I got up with a warm smile in my heart
And ready to face another beautiful day.

Siobhan Coates (9)
Our Lady of Pity RC Primary School

An Autumn Walk

Leaves are gently falling from the trees
Summer's gone, just like the buzzing bees.
It's autumn time and in the wood
I'm welly-walking through the sticky mud.
By the circle of logs, I saw a squirrel
Collecting nutty nuts from the ground in Wirral.
We followed the path around Royden Park
Not sad but happy until it was dark.

Daniel Arif Murphy (8)
Our Lady of Pity RC Primary School

Way Beyond The Sea

Way beyond the sea there's an island just for me,
Where monkeys speak words and there are dodo birds,
Oh, it seems to be on that island just for me.
Way beyond the sea, there's an island just for me,
Where elephants wear hats and there are wheels on bats,
Oh, it seems to be on that island just for me.

Mollie Eadsforth (9)
Our Lady of Pity RC Primary School

In London

Big Ben chimes loud and clear
Telling people the hour
Substantial evergreens
Sway lightly in the breeze.

The Thames is like a rippling radiant ribbon
Fluttering in the breeze
Big Ben's spire
Pierces the tranquil sky.

The fairy lights wind along the lamp post
Like a snake on the jungle floor
The bench's plank of wood
Is as brown as a bear's fur.

Luke Williams (10)
Our Lady of Pity RC Primary School

On A Mountain

In the distance lurks the trees
Blowing in the silent breeze
Up into the sky so high
On a mountain a man will lie.

On the rocks hard and stiff
But the man will not shift
He looks up to the sapphire glaze
To find himself just amazed.

His feet hurt and he's in pain
But he will not have shame
Because this place is the best
To look around and have a rest.

Katie Egan (10)
Our Lady of Pity RC Primary School

Christmas Gone Wrong

Mummy got a suit
Baby got a car
Brother got a dress
Grandad got a bra!

Daddy got some make-up
Nana got a tie
Sister got an Action Man
Everyone asked why?

Auntie got a football
Uncle got a rose
Why has this all happened?
Only Santa knows!

Hannah Rowlinson (8)
Our Lady of Pity RC Primary School

Excited

Excited is yellow
Excited smells like hot pepperoni pizza
Excited tastes like fizzy orange
Excited sounds like the tick-tock of a clock
Excited feels cosy and soft
Excited lives at home in my bed to keep it hot.

Ben Counsell (10)
Our Lady of Pity RC Primary School

B & B For A Flea

There once lived a girl called Bea
Who climbed up a crumbly old tree
A storm broke that day
And the tree gave way
And now it's a home for a flea.

Stephanie Burns (8)
Our Lady of Pity RC Primary School

The Globberslobber

The Globberslobber is springy, for he has no feet or toes
He just trundles along the ground giggling as he goes
Trying not to fall upon his clobby, cloppy nose
When the Globberslobber is hungry he gobbles up a fly
Slurping it into his mouth as they all fly by
As he goes rolling by, belching, burping, bouncing into the air
When the Globberslobber is tired he rolls into the stream
And floats upon the water where he passes his time to dream
To help him sleep he sucks a dummy till he hears a burp
from his mummy
He comes home and has some slug pie and now it's time
to say goodbye.

Luke Oliver Smith (9)
Our Lady of Pity RC Primary School

Bunny Eggs

Easter bunny, Easter bunny, won't you bring an egg for me
Easter eggs, Easter eggs, Easter eggs all for me
White and fluffy bunny in our house
White and fluffy bunny as quiet as a mouse
Little white bunny jumping all around
Up and down and landing on the ground
Chocolate wrappers all glowing and colourful
But when unravelled even more wonderful
We end our Easter Day by saying
Thank you bunny for our scrumptious day.

Ally Whyte (9)
Our Lady of Pity RC Primary School

Luxurious London

Tall crooked trees loom over the paved ground
Like a lion standing over its prey
Grey buildings stand tall like soldiers to attention
Glittering fairies dance happily across blue ribbons of sea
Violins sound in the distance and make a noise like a wondrous
bird singing
The calm sky is an endless, enchanted piece of blue string
Big Ben is a sword piercing the peaceful blue sky
The crisp wind makes up a whirlwind of magical crimson leaves
The blinding sun shines on the rough jade hilltops
Black clouds stream for long boats
Bridges are like the wide-open mouths of a hungry giant
A large chubby squirrel climbs up the tree in fear of creatures below
As birds swoop to catch their prey.

Joshua Byrne (10)
Our Lady of Pity RC Primary School

It's A Summer Day

Everyone's at the beach today having an amazing time
There are buckets and spades, swimming in waves and rays
of beauty and shine
The sun is shining, no person is whining because the holidays
have just begun
People are screaming, the sun is beaming and everyone's having fun
The sea is a blast; you can swim very fast in the radiant mix of blue
There is also some emerald and flashes of sunshine that come
within the sea too
Now I have explained about summer and all its love and wonder
But as the sun sets we get ready for . . . *autumn!*

Lewis Egan (8)
Our Lady of Pity RC Primary School

The Light In Your Eyes Is Mine

The light in your eyes is the love in your eyes
And the love in your eyes is mine
So the love in my eyes meets the light in your eyes
To wine and dine through time
And when time has expired
And the light has expired
The love will still burn within
To light up new eyes
Meet the love in your eyes
Through time and time and time.

Ryan Crane (9)
Our Lady of Pity RC Primary School

View Of Life

A tall man sits on a huge jagged rock
A huge, long, foggy cloud floats getting closer
Totally tranquil the grass is pure jade
The really vivid sky fading behind the foggy crawling cloud
A large cliff is standing not wrecked but in total stillness
The river stays full of water with the wind blowing the current
The tiny houses stay standing like Lego
The lush green bushes get pushed by the wind
The river is pure purple.

Adam Sadler (9)
Our Lady of Pity RC Primary School

Hope

Hope is the colour of a rose
It smells like a bottle of rich delicious perfume
Hope has the taste of creamy chocolate
It sounds like the wind is carrying a floaty dreamy butterfly
The feel of it is comforting and heart-warming
Hope lives in your heart.

Katie Murphy (9)
Our Lady of Pity RC Primary School

Happiness And Sadness

Happiness
Happiness looks like a golden sun
Happiness feels like a cuddly teddy bear
Happiness smells like a beautiful red rose
Happiness tastes like a piece of cake.

Sadness
Sadness looks like a cold wall
Sadness feels like a storm of rain
Sadness smells like a rotten egg
Sadness tastes bitter.

Alex Toland (7)
SS Peter & Paul Catholic Primary School, Wallasey

All About Anger

Anger is red like red-hot chillies
It tastes like hot boiled apple made in a frying pan
It smells like you talking very fast to your mum
It sounds like a volcano about to explode
Anger is very bleak.

Mara Vangoffon (7)
SS Peter & Paul Catholic Primary School, Wallasey

Anger

Anger is like very hot chilli
Anger feels like your friends have made you look silly
And you just want them crushed
It sounds like a volcano has been mushed
It smells like dirty feet
It tastes like something you wouldn't want to eat
And that's the reason I don't like to feel like this.

Ana McSorley (8)
SS Peter & Paul Catholic Primary School, Wallasey

Happiness

Happiness is like the brightest beam of sunshine shining down
on the Earth
It feels loving, like a snuggly, warm and furry teddy bear
Happiness smells like melting chocolate, oozing off
a chocolate fountain
It tastes as delicious as a hot blackcurrant drink, sipped slowly
on a cold night.

Ellie English (7)
SS Peter & Paul Catholic Primary School, Wallasey

Loneliness

Loneliness is like the colour you have been waiting to see
It tastes like emptiness
It sounds like a silent whistle
It feels like spending Christmas all by yourself
It looks like someone standing at a bus stop on a rainy day
For me loneliness is all these things and more.

Joseph Bowly (8)
SS Peter & Paul Catholic Primary School, Wallasey

Fear

Fear sounds like a wolf howling,
Fear looks like a lion prowling,
Fear smells like a damp musty night,
Fear feels like a bad, bad bite,
But most of all fear tastes like the fierce howling sea.

Katharine Quinn (9)
SS Peter & Paul Catholic Primary School, Wallasey

Happiness

Happiness feels like you are magic
Happiness smells like when your dinner is in the oven
Happiness tastes like apple crumble
Happiness looks like a red rose
Happiness is orange
Happiness sounds like best friends talking to each other.

Luke Wellens (8)
SS Peter & Paul Catholic Primary School, Wallasey

Happiness

Happiness is like fizzy lemonade on a hot summer's day
When I'm with my friends and the games that we play
Like a family day out when we go to the park
Or visit the aquarium and look at a shark
When we play games and I'm in the lead
Happiness is just what I need.

Phoebe Jones (8)
SS Peter & Paul Catholic Primary School, Wallasey

Fear

Fear is like being bullied
Fear is being bullied
Fear smells like seaweed
Fear looks like you're going to be bullied.

Aidan McCulloch (8)
SS Peter & Paul Catholic Primary School, Wallasey

Sadness

Sadness tastes like mouldy bread
Sadness looks like a lonely girl
Sadness sounds like hollow footsteps
Sadness feels like an empty world
Sadness is blue like the big blue ocean
Sadness smells like wilting flowers.

Ellie Regan (9)
SS Peter & Paul Catholic Primary School, Wallasey

Love

Love smells like a rose
Love is a warm happy feeling
Love tastes like hot chocolate on a cold wet day
Love is being part of a very happy family
Love is what you feel for your mum and dad.

Katie Gillespie (8)
SS Peter & Paul Catholic Primary School, Wallasey

Love

Love is beautiful and she's got a beautiful smell
When you look after her, she will grow
When you don't nurse her she wilts like a flower.

Nicole Stasik (8)
SS Peter & Paul Catholic Primary School, Wallasey

Young Writers Information

We hope you have enjoyed reading this book - and that you will continue to enjoy it in the coming years.

If you like reading and writing poetry drop us a line, or give us a call, and we'll send you a free information pack.

Alternatively if you would like to order further copies of this book or any of our other titles, then please give us a call or log onto our website at www.youngwriters.co.uk

Young Writers Information
Remus House
Coltsfoot Drive
Peterborough
PE2 9JX

(01733) 890066